Putting on a Show

by Karra McFarlane
illustrated by Sam Loman

OXFORD
UNIVERSITY PRESS
AUSTRALIA & NEW ZEALAND

It was the start of the holidays. Leo, Kavan and Ava were in Ava's garden.

"What shall we do?" asked Ava.

"Let's put on a show!" said Leo.
"We could perform it for our families tomorrow."

"What about a circus show?" said Kavan.

"Good thinking!" said Ava.

They made invites asking people
to come to the show.

Then it was time for some circus training!

Leo found some beanbags. He decided he would juggle.

It was harder than it looked. Leo kept dropping the beanbags.

Ava found an old baton in her little sister's dressing-up box.

"Can I borrow this, Violet?" Ava asked.

Ava began to twirl the baton.

It flew from her hand and hit her shoulder.

"Ouch!" she shrieked.

"I quite like speaking aloud," Kavan said to himself. "I'm going to be the ringmaster."

However, Kavan could not think of what to say or do.

11

"Don't give up!" called Violet.
"I'm sure the show will be perfect."

Leo, Ava and Kavan kept going.

The following afternoon...

Ava, Leo and Kavan were full of dread.
It was time to perform.

Leo put on the music.

The children went on...

Ava did not drop her baton.

Leo's juggling was perfect.

Kavan made the best ringmaster ever.

All the training had paid off.

People clapped and cheered.
Cameras flashed.

The show was a big success!

"What shall we do tomorrow?" asked Ava, with a smile.

"I would like a rest!" said Kavan.

"Me too!" said Leo.